Thinning Your Life

Work Less, Do More, Be Wealthy

The Ultimate Investment Part 3

A Business Fable

See other works by H. Bradley Stucki at www.amazon.com/author/hbstucki. Free downloads are often available. Click "Follow" on his Author Page for updates on new releases.

Chapter One

Dan rolled over, his bleary eyes finding the clock on his nightstand: 3:38 AM. "Swell," he mumbled, willing his body to relax. But relaxation wouldn't come. His mind darted between the day's concerns and the conversation he'd have to have with Mandie this morning—telling her he wouldn't make it to their family vacation for yet another day. He could only hope to salvage the last two days of their first family trip to Disneyland.

The announcement that he needed to stay behind to complete a rush order hadn't gone over well. He couldn't turn down such a large order from a new customer—one that could bring steady monthly income. If his metal-wire figurines sold well in this chain of hotel gift shops, it could boost his production by 15%, along with his income.

His decision had sparked their first major argument in... he couldn't even remember how long. Mandie, typically supportive and gracious, had erupted. How dare he abandon his family! How dare he put his precious *business* ahead of their vacation plans! This was their first family vacation in years! Was he married to his business? Was he the father of his little figurines? Would one more account really make that much difference? And if they were going to be such a good customer, wouldn't they understand waiting a few more days?

Her outburst had shocked him, revealing a deep frustration he hadn't realized existed. Instead of backing down like a wise husband should have, he'd fired right back. He was doing it all for his family! Did she think he enjoyed working fifteen-hour days? Did she think he liked missing the kids' activities? Did she think he enjoyed the constant pressure of producing enough every single day to avoid another financial crisis?

It seemed longer than just a year since they'd almost lost their house. They'd pulled through at the last minute, working together. Since then, they'd prospered. Dan had maintained his large accounts and gift shops, expanding as his product gained recognition. He now supplied 34 shops and three chains—potentially four, if he could fill this order. Business was thriving, but it consumed every moment of his time.

His financial stress had decreased only to be replaced by the pressure of maintaining and growing the business. No wonder Mandie had snapped. She'd felt the pressure too, holding it in just as he had.

To compensate for the long hours and missed events, he'd promised Mandie and the kids a family vacation after the Christmas rush. The year had been good enough that Mandie felt they could splurge on their dream trip. The kids had sacrificed too—they deserved this reward.

Disneyland, the dream of every child young and old, was perfect. Mandie had admitted she wanted to go as badly as the kids did. At the time, Dan hadn't foreseen any problems. Orders would slow down, and he could work ahead on inventory. He'd informed his main customers, and everything seemed set. Then came the call: a buyer for a chain of hotel gift shops had seen his product and needed it immediately. The problem? Dan's small inventory was already committed. He'd have to create new figurines to ship. If he worked longer hours, he could finish in a day and join his family. But Mandie hadn't seen it that way.

What choice did he have? He'd already committed. He couldn't back out now. Didn't Mandie understand? This would help them reach their goals by adding another substantial, steady customer. Then things would ease up, and the pressure would decrease.

So Mandie and the kids had left without him, the new minivan filled with luggage, snacks, and electronic devices. Dan had watched them drive away before heading to his garage workshop. But calls had come in, and issues had arisen that needed immediate attention. Questions about the product from other potential customers he couldn't ignore meant he hadn't completed as much of the order as planned. It would take an extra day. This time he'd turn off his phone and avoid checking emails. He'd already announced he wouldn't be available. He just had to stick to that plan, finish the order, and join his family.

Dan had worked until midnight before crawling into bed. He'd made good progress but still wasn't finished. He needed the extra day to complete the order—and that was if he ignored his phone and emails. He'd fallen asleep as soon as his head hit the pillow around 12:45 AM, but by 3:38, he was wide awake, his mind racing with concerns, especially about Mandie.

Would Mandie have cooled down by now—especially since she was at Disneyland? Somehow Dan doubted it. She'd probably be angrier because of his absence. Mandie was fiercely protective of *family time.* That was her domain every bit as much as the business was his.

"How did it get this bad?" Dan asked the ceiling. "I thought being my own boss would allow me to take time off whenever I wanted." That fantasy had proved far from reality. Being his own boss tied him down even more than working for someone else. In his previous job, he'd had colleagues to cover for him during vacation. Now, there was no one. If he didn't work, he didn't get paid. The orders wouldn't fill themselves.

There was no use lying in bed. He knew sleep wouldn't return until his mind calmed. But he was too exhausted to work in the garage on the figurines. He needed at least a couple more hours of rest before another marathon building session.

He had completed just over half the order, tackling the most complicated figurines first. Now only the routine ones remained. Boxing and shipping didn't require much time or concentration, so he'd left those tasks for last.

Sliding out of bed, he put on his slippers and made his way downstairs. Walking into the kitchen for a drink of water, he stopped. The wooden plaque on the wall caught the dim light from the hallway—Mandie's careful hand-lettering, the words she'd burned into the wood the year they almost lost everything. Beneath them, the paper note she'd taped on later, its edges curling slightly now.

Invest your time. Don't just spend it.
Follow the Path, Live the Dream.

Dan looked away. Those words had saved them once. Tonight they felt like an accusation. He was investing all of his time—every waking hour—in the business. And the people those words were meant to protect were at Disneyland without him.

He kept walking to the family room and settled into his recliner. He picked up the TV remote. Maybe some mindless television would quiet his thoughts enough for sleep to return. At least he could catch a few winks in the recliner before starting again.

He was really dreading that phone call to Mandie.

Chapter Two

Dan sat in the darkened room, the television's flickering glow casting strange dancing shadows as he surfed channels, searching for something to distract him from his worries. He settled into the new, overstuffed recliner Mandie had insisted they get—his personal reward for how hard he'd worked to save their home. The truth was, Mandie had worked every bit as hard, if not harder, taking on the school job to keep them afloat while he built their business.

Mandie hadn't wanted anything except... Dan groaned again... the family vacation. It was the only thing she'd asked for after all they'd been through. *Dan had let her down.* The enormity of what he'd really done crashed over him. Now he understood why Mandie had exploded when he'd asked for just one more day. In her mind, it had been a betrayal.

Disappointment in himself washed over Dan. Tears moistened his eyes as the television blared unheard into the darkness. He'd been so focused on his work that he hadn't considered its effect on Mandie and the children. He'd assumed they'd understand he was doing it all for them. The sacrifice of long hours, hard work, and missed events—it was all for his family.

But was it really? Was it more about building a successful business? Yes, he worried about providing for his family and finally earning enough to enjoy some of life's finer things, but was the cost becoming too high?

Frustration seeped through his sorrow. How did others manage? He felt like he was working himself to death, while others seemed to glide through life earning fortunes. What was he missing? Dan's sadness began turning to anger.

It had started with that dream! That Opportunity Tree dream, where the fruit had tasted so delicious, so convincing that he'd believed his life would become paradise if he could just reach that certain point...

And he had reached it. He'd tasted that fruit when he and Mandie saved their home through their hard work with his designed, crafted, and sold figurines. It had indeed tasted delicious!

And there was the Ultimate Investment that had started it all—Elizabeth's clues, her letter, her refusal to give him the answer because she loved him too much to make it easy. He thought of Sheldon, showing up at six in the morning with two thermoses of coffee, doing the only thing he knew how to do: looking at a thing carefully and wanting to make it better. Elizabeth had warned him about so many things. But she hadn't warned him about this—that the answer, once found, could become its own trap. She'd told him to invest his time, not spend it. She never said what to do when investing becomes indistinguishable from spending. But now he was investing too much! *"Invest a large amount of your Ultimate Investment in your family or you'll lose everything else of real value."*

Things had gotten out of balance. The delicious taste of success was souring as the hours mounted and tension with Mandie grew.

Dan saw it clearly now. Mandie had grown quieter. She'd stopped commenting and had even stopped inviting him to events, he realized. He'd mistaken it for support, thinking she was avoiding disturbing him. Now he saw it differently. Her attitude toward him had changed, had cooled—something he couldn't quite define but felt deeply.

Then it clicked: Mandie's extreme anger at his delayed vacation departure. She'd been biding her time, hoping this vacation, this family time would break Dan free from his workaholic life.

Mandie was counting on this trip to change things. And Dan had casually dismissed it—like he'd dismissed so many other small but significant moments.

This isn't helping, Dan thought to himself, finally trying to quell his frustration and sorrow to focus on whatever television station he'd landed on. He'd been mindlessly pushing the remote control, flipping through channels without registering what was playing.

"In this episode of The Master Arborist, we'll discuss the importance of pruning the tree and thinning the fruit. Work less and get more harvest." Dan tilted his head, realizing he'd stopped on the agricultural channel.

"What's this?" he whispered. Something about that last bit the announcer had said struck him. Working less and getting a greater harvest? And it involved trees and fruit... *Is this a coincidence?* Something deep within told Dan it wasn't. He remembered Mandie's teasing recitation of the ancient Chinese proverb: "When a student is ready, a teacher will appear." Was this going to mean something? Dan was definitely ready.

He grabbed the remote, careful not to change the channel. Switching on the lamp beside his chair, he fumbled to find the DVR button. He had to record this!

#

An hour later, tears of relief streamed down Dan's face. *This is the answer!* Though he didn't know exactly how to apply it yet, at least he had found direction. Mandie would want to see this too! She would help—as she always had.

One thing was certain: Dan was going on vacation! And he wouldn't wait until filling that order. He was leaving right away, regardless of the account.

After ensuring the DVR had recorded the show, he went to the garage. He pulled his wallet from the counter where he'd left it and flipped it open to find Carson's contact information he'd scrawled on a note and put in his wallet so he wouldn't lose it. As he thumbed past his driver's license, he saw the folded note slipped partway out—three lines in Mandie's careful handwriting, creased and softened from years of carrying. He felt the pull to unfold it, the way he always did, and gave in. The words looked back at him in the dim garage light. He read them slowly, then folded the note and tucked it back behind the license. It stung tonight more than usual. He set the contact information beside the keyboard and opened his email. Typing, he apologized and let the buyer know that there was going to be a week's delay in getting his order out. To compensate, he would reduce this first order by 8%. He hoped that was acceptable but if not, would understand if they canceled their order.

He switched off the computer, paused, then turned off his phone too. He headed upstairs to dress and finish packing, too excited to sleep. Rather than call Mandie, he would surprise her at the hotel.

Saying he was sorry... for everything... would be better in person, especially when she heard what he'd just learned.

The Opportunity Tree wasn't just a dream! And the Ultimate Investment is priceless!

Chapter Three

Dan and Mandie sat nestled together on the family room couch, the space dim with only a single lamp illuminating their evening. They had just returned from their Disneyland trip, where they'd created wonderful memories together. Dan felt profound relief that the warmth had returned between them. His decision to surprise Mandie at the hotel rather than make that dreaded postponement call had been the right choice. Though his arrival had initially been met with frost, spending time with the kids in the park—phone deliberately shut off—had begun to thaw the tension. When Dan proposed extending their stay by an extra day, the children's cheers had brought tears to Mandie's eyes, and their world had righted itself again.

During the quiet moments of their vacation, Dan had shared his revelation with her, hoping she would help him determine their next steps. Her eyes had twinkled with their familiar light as she agreed, though he noticed a hint of reservation. He could sense her worry that this change of heart might not last.

Now, with the children tucked safely in bed, Dan prepared to show Mandie what he believed would transform their lives. Despite his certainty that she would understand, nervous energy coursed through him. She had to see it too!

Dan switched on the television and started the DVR recording. As the program played, he found himself watching Mandie's reactions almost as much as the show itself...

#

When the program ended, Dan turned off the power and faced his wife. "What do you think? Is it what I was telling you? Do you think it applies to our business?"

Mandie remained quiet for a moment, her gaze fixed intently on Dan's eyes. "I think it *is* a message," she said finally. "Whether it's coincidence doesn't matter—we just need to understand how to apply it. And I believe this goes beyond the business. It's crucial for us individually and as a family. Really, it's something everyone should consider."

"I agree!" Relief flooded through Dan. "I'm so glad you see it too. I have some ideas I'd like to share with you."

"Before we do that," Mandie suggested, "we should each take time to think deeply about this and make notes. It will help us process everything more clearly." She rose and walked to the kitchen, returning moments later with a notepad, a pencil, and her manila folder—the same one that had started as a detective's file hunting for E.M.A. and had grown, over the years, into a compendium of their journey. She set it on the couch beside her.

After settling back against Dan and drawing his arm around her shoulders, she wrote at the top of the pad: "Pruning and Thinning; The Benjamin Family plan for nourishing life!"

"Wow!" Dan exclaimed. "You aren't thinking small."

"I don't think we can afford to think small," Mandie replied. "It may seem simple on the surface, but in my heart, I feel this could become something extraordinary." She opened the folder and pulled out a small leather-bound notebook—Elizabeth's business journal, the one Michael had given her. "Elizabeth nearly destroyed her company by trying to do too much, too fast. She wrote about it in here. We're making the same mistake, Dan—just from the other side. She grew too fast. We're working too hard. Same problem, different symptom."

She paused thoughtfully before continuing. "The show focused on growing fruit trees. That connects directly to your dream of the

Opportunity Tree. Since it was a fruit tree, the same principles would apply."

"That's exactly what I was thinking," Dan smiled, encouraging her insights.

"The show emphasized that to achieve the best harvest with minimal effort, you must prune and thin your fruit trees annually. Following this practice leads to the largest yield and the sweetest fruit."

"That's right," Dan confirmed, restraining his enthusiasm to let Mandie's thoughts flow.

"Pruning is about removing branches that won't produce efficiently—whether they're overcrowded and stealing strength from a main branch, growing in the wrong direction, or would be out of reach during harvest time."

"Yes," Dan agreed, his eyes sparkling with recognition. She was seeing the same vision he had!

"The goal is giving branches space and strength to reach their full potential. Even with fewer branches, the remaining ones become far more productive than if every branch had been preserved."

Mandie carefully recorded these thoughts on her pad.

"Then there's thinning," she continued. "When budding fruit begins to appear on the remaining limbs, you remove some of it, creating space between each immature fruit. This gives each piece room to grow and draw strength from both limb and roots."

Dan couldn't contain himself any longer. "I've watched the show twice now. They removed about half or more of the budding fruit, letting it fall to the ground. At first, it seemed wasteful, but then the arborist explained how the remaining fruit thrives without competition for nourishment. Leaving everything on would result in stunted, bitter fruit. Too much growth would ruin the entire harvest."

"And what I'm realizing," Mandie interjected, "is that this applies to individuals and families just as much as it applies to your business. It aligns perfectly with the Ultimate Investment. Remember the clues? The principles?"

Dan pondered this. "You're right, as usual."

Mandie fell silent, then reached back to switch off the lamp behind the couch. Darkness enveloped the room.

"I want to sleep on this," she murmured, snuggling closer to Dan. "This is something I've been searching for too. I need to let it sink in before we discuss how to apply it to every area." She placed her hand on his chest. "The message is for both of us."

Chapter Four

Dan and Mandie sat in a conference room of their local library, a place that had been a source of discovery for them before and would be again. Dan noted the symbolism of their return. Once more, they were hoping to find solutions to their challenges.

Mandie had reserved the room in advance to ensure they could talk freely without interruption.

Unlike their previous visit, when they'd searched through books for clues to the Ultimate Investment, today they carried notes about how to *prune* and *thin* their lives.

They settled at a round table, notepads and pens before them, their jackets draped over their chair backs. Dan wore jeans and a t-shirt, a marked change from his former shirt-and-tie workdays. Mandie, true to form, wore neat slacks and a colorful blouse—not expensive, but tasteful and well-put-together. She always looked polished.

The library had just opened, with only a few other patrons about. Some wandered past and glanced through the glass door. *Like being in a fishbowl*, Dan thought. Funny how he'd never noticed that during their previous visits. *Must have been too preoccupied.* This session wasn't about saving their home; the atmosphere felt more relaxed. In fact, Dan felt optimistic. He hoped Mandie shared his outlook.

Mandie began, "You know, the more I've considered this, the more convinced I am it's exactly what we need. This concept of pruning and thinning—I've never thought about it before, but it fits perfectly. If we apply it to our lives, both individually and as a family, it creates space for the truly important things to flourish."

"I agree," Dan said. "And thank you for thinking about the family. I've been focused mainly on the business aspects. But if this works out, I hope my pruning and thinning will benefit everyone. I want more time with all of you—without sacrificing our income or stability."

Mandie smiled warmly, placing her hand over his where it rested on the table. "It all leads to the same goal. Why don't you go first and share your thoughts?"

"I'll start with pruning," Dan said, pulling his notebook closer. He used his pen as a pointer to track his ideas. "First, I reviewed all our customers. Most are excellent—they order by email, I fill it, ship it, and they send payment. No problems, no hassles. Those are our best customers.

"Then there are the difficult ones. They order, I deliver, but getting payment requires constant follow-up. Thankfully, these aren't our major accounts—one medium-sized customer and three smaller ones.

"We also have several small clients who order just three or four figurines monthly. They insist on phone orders and always haggle over prices. Or they claim damage upon delivery and demand discounts.

"I know the figurines aren't damaged—they never want replacements, just price reductions. They're simply angling for better deals.

"I believe I need to *prune* my customer base. Make room for the strongest branches to grow in the right direction. This should free up time to nurture other branches that can bear more fruit."

Mandie smiled at his tree analogy. It fit perfectly. "That's good thinking. What specific actions will you take?"

"I'm implementing three changes: minimum orders of five units to optimize shipping, prepayment requirements for chronically late payers, and a return-for-replacement policy on damage claims. These problem accounts represent less than one percent of our volume—but when I calculated the time I spend managing them, it came to seventeen percent. Seventeen percent of my Ultimate Investment, spent on unproductive customers."

"Wow," Mandie said thoughtfully. "Saving 17% of your time is significant, especially if you *reinvest* it for higher yields."

Dan grinned. "You're sexy when you talk business."

"But I'm right and you know it," Mandie smiled. "Now about *thinning...*"

"Right here," Dan said, turning to his next page. "For thinning, I examined my use of time—the Ultimate Investment. I identified where I'm most productive and looked for areas to thin out less productive activities.

"It relates to the 80/20 rule—the Pareto Principle, I always heard about when I was working for Amsco. Basically, 80 percent of results come from 20 percent of efforts. Similarly, 80 percent of problems come from 20 percent of customers. While the numbers aren't exact, the proportion holds surprisingly true.

"My most valuable time goes into designing figurines. It's also what brings me the greatest satisfaction. Our business exists because of these unique designs, yet I spend less than 10% of my time creating them. Assembly—after the initial design—consumes most of my time now. That's something I could train others to do.

"If I can find people to efficiently construct the figurines, I can focus more on design and developing relationships with *good* customers."

"So you're considering hiring employees?" Mandie asked.

"Well... yes," Dan admitted. "It seems the only way to thin my time down to focus on my most productive work—that crucial 20 percent."

"Where would they work?" Mandie questioned. "Would you need to rent business space?"

"That's the challenging part," Dan sighed. "I'm running the numbers. With employees, we'd need workspace—which means renting or buying property. It could be basic since we don't need a storefront, but we'd still need significantly increased volume to cover that overhead."

Mandie considered this quietly. "What about this?" she suggested. "Hire independent assemblers and pay per piece. They work from their homes, eliminating the need for rental space. Plus, you avoid employee management issues. You provide materials and designs; they deliver finished products and receive payment. Their earnings depend on their productivity. If their work quality or speed doesn't meet standards, you can end the agreement or reduce their workload."

"That's brilliant. How did you develop that idea?"

"I read a lot—we are in a library, after all," she smiled. "I've been studying *systems* for streamlining work and improving process flow. That should be part of your thinning plan. Good systems maintain quality while reducing costs and freeing up *time*."

Dan bowed his head, smiling. "You've been thinking about this for a while, haven't you?"

"Since your hours got so long. But I held back because I saw how stressed you were. I could just hear you saying, 'Training someone would take as long as doing it myself.'"

Dan chuckled. "And now?"

"Now you're less stressed. You're ready to hear it." Mandie's smile softened the observation.

"And I know your first potential assembler," she added.

"Oh? Who?" Dan asked.

"Remember that young man who worked with the con man who tried to steal our business? He did excellent work copying your pieces. Maybe he deserves a chance at honest work. It would be similar to what he did before, and you said his quality was good."

"I don't know," Dan hesitated.

"Listen. I'll contact the detective and reach out. At least give him a chance. What's the risk? You know his work quality and speed. He probably needs income, plus he has restitution to pay as part of his sentence. It seems like a win-win situation."

"Okay, okay." Dan held up his hands. "I'll give him a chance if he's willing." He paused, then added, "Actually, I need someone quick. The orders are piling up again. I could use the help."

"Now what about you?" Dan asked. "We've covered the business side. Let's hear what you've been thinking about."

Mandie scooted her chair closer to the table and opened her floral notepad to the first page.

"I started by examining everything I was doing, then identified what I felt was most important to accomplish—primarily raising the kids and developing myself. I want to pursue more education. And of course," she batted her eyes at Dan, "taking care of my 'dear' husband ranks right up there."

"Thanks a lot," Dan said. "I appreciate the consideration."

"Anyway," Mandie continued, "I listed everything I do weekly. Anything that didn't contribute to those main priorities, I started *pruning*, striking it from the list. It was astounding how much was there. My tree had become seriously overgrown. Remember how stressed and flustered I'd be some evenings? I'm hoping that becomes rare now.

"Most of what I've eliminated are things others guilted me into doing by making me feel bad for not 'helping out.' The exciting part is what I can now *add* to the list. I'll still help others, but I'm going to be more selective and master the magic word, *no*.

"Quality *family time* is essential. From now on we're eating dinner together at least four nights weekly—including you, mister! Plus, we're having family night once or twice a week with no outside activities—just *family* activities.

"And you and I," Mandie arched an eyebrow at Dan, "are going on a weekly date, without the kids. And no discussing children—or business."

"Whoa," Dan said. "That's serious... but good! I like it."

"I'm pruning away the bad branches so the good can grow stronger. I want our family to be our greatest harvest," Mandie said. "They deserve a giant share of our Ultimate Investment!"

"Amen!" Dan agreed. He felt profound gratitude for Mandie's devotion to him and their children. He realized what a fool he'd been. Mandie was his greatest ally, and he made a silent commitment to always cherish and treat her as such.

"Next," Mandie said, flipping her notepad page. "I examined the kids' schedules. I hadn't realized how overwhelmed they'd become with activities they want to do and are expected to do. No wonder I was going crazy trying to manage it all.

"I listed their weekly activities, considering what would be most important for their growth as productive people." Mandie turned to Dan with a smile. "Dare I say, *good fruit*?"

Dan rolled his eyes playfully.

"I began eliminating activities that didn't contribute to their core development. And relax," Mandie held up a hand, "I didn't cut out all the fun. I kept plenty of enjoyable activities—just the ones that lead to productive ends. I even preserved some free time where they can choose their activities—even watching TV, though hopefully less of it."

"Sounds perfect," Dan said. "I support this completely. Just give me the list of *prohibited* activities so I won't cave when they ask. We don't want a good Dad, bad Mom situation." He referenced the classic 'good cop vs. bad cop' scenario.

"Thanks, Honey," Mandie said. "Yes, I'll share the list. But I don't want to over-program them. I want them to recognize the value of their own *Ultimate Investment*. We should teach them what we've learned, hoping they can incorporate these principles earlier than we did.

"It won't happen automatically, though. We'll need to stay firm. Looking at their friends' schedules, it's incredible how structured children's lives are now. Remember our childhood? Didn't we have abundant free time just to play?

"We didn't have tablets, digital players, video games, and endless TV shows. Now there's every league imaginable—baseball, basketball, football, soccer, even hockey. Plus lessons—singing, dance, swimming, piano..."

"I get it," Dan said, raising his hands in surrender. After a thoughtful pause, he added, "The kids really are overbooked. I understand why you see the need to prune. I'm exhausted just thinking about you managing their schedules. So, what about *thinning*?"

Mandie turned another page in her notepad.

"Thinning proved more challenging. It's about reducing growth on a branch so the best fruit has strength to reach its full potential.

"I evaluated the remaining activities and decided to pare them down to their essential elements that make them valuable.

"For instance, when preparing my Sunday School lessons, instead of spending time on elaborate handouts and treats, I'll focus on studying the material more deeply to make it more meaningful for my students.

"With everything else, I'm concentrating on the core purpose rather than the surrounding presentation. This way, I emphasize the meaning and intent rather than superficial appearances.

"I think we've become a *show* society, emphasizing *flash* and *production* over meaningful content. Life's deeper significance is fading. People receive constant stimulation without being *filled* with anything substantial."

Mandie paused, then added, "Elizabeth wrote about this in her notebook—how she had to learn to stop decorating and start designing. The decorations were what people praised, but the design was what made the dress last. I've been decorating my life instead of designing it."

"Wow!" Dan exclaimed. "That's profound. You've identified something important. Consider what we watch on TV—it's entertaining, but what's the value? Not to criticize TV entirely, since entertainment matters, but look at today's news. It's mostly argument and spin rather than actual information. Lots of noise and spectacle, but how much truly matters?

"I need to apply this beyond business too. Like you've done, I should list everything and focus on the core elements, ensuring I do them well. That way, I'll grow as a person and have the *time* to make it happen."

"I've been thinking," Mandie said. "We've been blessed with everything we truly need, including *time*. By pruning and thinning our lives, we'll have more of it to maximize our Ultimate Investment."

"You are brilliant, my dear," Dan said, pulling Mandie to her feet and embracing her. The library patrons peering through the study room door didn't matter.

After a moment, Mandie stepped back. "By the way, I realized we need more insight about pruning and thinning, and I discovered that the Master Arborist from that show lives nearby. Would you mind if I contacted him for a consultation? I think we could learn valuable applications beyond what the TV show covered. We could share how we're applying the principles and see what he might add. I have a feeling it could be significant."

"You're really embracing this," Dan said, pleased that she was taking things even further than he had. "By all means, see if he'll meet with us."

Chapter Five

"I'm sorry you feel that way," Dan spoke into the phone. "Your inconsistent payment history has forced me to implement prepay status on your account." He listened to the response—the same excuses he'd heard twice already this week. The clients were upset about the prepayment requirement, threatening to stop ordering. They could at least be civil about it. This call, however, was turning decidedly unpleasant.

"Again," Dan interrupted the tirade, "once you've re-established credit over a six-month period, your credit privileges will be restored..."

More words erupted, rising in volume until Dan had to hold the phone away from his ear.

Mandie entered the garage workshop and assessed the situation. Dan offered a wry smile. She held up a glass of lemonade, and he responded with a finger—*one minute*, he mouthed.

"I'm sorry, but the new policy is final. Arguing won't change it. Oh, excuse me, I have another call coming in." Dan winked at Mandie. "If you reconsider ordering, you have the website address with all the forms. Enclose a check with your order, and you can continue receiving merchandise. Have a good day." He hung up, took a deep breath, rubbed his eyes, and stretched. A dull ache in his left shoulder had been nagging him for a few days—probably from hunching over the workbench. He rolled it out and reached for the lemonade.

"Was that as bad as it looked?" Mandie asked, placing the lemonade on a coaster on Dan's desk.

"About what I expected from that customer." He lifted the glass and took a long drink. "Getting yelled at is thirsty work. I hope this new policy isn't cutting our throat. So far, everyone I've put on prepay claims they'll stop ordering. I know I said we could manage without them, but our margin for error shrinks with each lost account."

"Remember the *pruning* and *thinning* principles. We'll be able to focus more energy on growing better fruit," Mandie reminded him. "Haven't you been able to do more design work since bringing on the independent contractors for assembly?"

"I have," Dan admitted. "I've created several new sports figurines and added them to the website. Though I haven't placed them in any new shops yet, our current retailers like the additions."

"It'll come," Mandie assured him. "You're experienced in sales. Didn't you tell me it was a numbers game? Get in front of enough target customers, and the sales will follow."

"You're right, as usual, my dear." Dan took her hand. "It's just hard to stay positive after being chewed out. Having you here helps me bounce back faster."

"How are the assemblers working out?" Mandie asked, shifting the subject.

"They're fantastic. Darrel—the young man Raymond Chandler recruited to copy our figurines after we turned down his deal—is our star performer. He's grateful for the work, especially since it counts toward his restitution. Job hunting had been tough for him, so he's really applying himself. He's handling about half our volume now, and his quality is excellent. He's even faster than I am!

"He's also proposed some design ideas I really like. We'll develop them for the website, and I've promised him design royalties for each sale. He's quite excited about that."

"That's wonderful!" Mandie exclaimed. "What about the others?"

"We have two women and an older gentleman," Dan explained. "The women do great work and appreciate being able to work from home while their kids are in school. It fits their schedules perfectly. Though not as intensive as Darrel, their work is solid. They sometimes gather at one home to work together."

"And the older gentleman? Brantly?"

I mainly use him for building inventory. Between Walt's local connections and Paul still handling our West Coast festival and specialty shop distribution, we're covering more ground than I ever could alone. Paul was the one who first saw the potential—put five figurines on a table and sold them all in a day. Without him, none of this exists.

"However, Brantly's brought an unexpected benefit—he's convinced several local shops to stock our figurines, increasing our volume. He says he can get us into more shops. Apparently, he's quite the networker and knows many business owners. I'm paying him a bonus for each new shop, which works well for everyone."

"So there are bright spots?" Mandie smiled, squeezing his hand. "Oh! I almost forgot why I came out here. I've arranged a meeting with the Master Arborist from the show. He's coming tomorrow afternoon. Will that work for you?"

"It will," Dan nodded. "With the extra help, my schedule's much more flexible. I'm really starting to enjoy this business again."

"Just ignore the negativity. Prune it away and move forward." Mandie leaned down to kiss him, then playfully pinched his cheek. "Now get back to work!" She headed back into the house.

Chapter Six

"Welcome!" Mandie ushered the visitor into their cozy front room. "This is my husband, Dan."

"Pleased to meet you," the man said. "Please call me Hank." Tall and lean, in his mid-sixties, he wore a pale blue button-down denim shirt and Levi's. "Should I remove my boots? They should be clean," he offered with a gracious smile. Dan noticed his weathered face and sun-kissed cheeks—clear evidence of a life spent outdoors.

"No need," Dan said, shaking his hand. He immediately warmed to the man's quiet confidence. There was no pretension, no airs—just genuine down-to-earth sincerity.

"Thanks for coming. I'm Mandie, we spoke on the phone." Hank shook her hand with another warm smile.

"Thank you for inviting me. What you described was intriguing. I couldn't help but be curious about your request."

"Please, sit," Mandie gestured to the recliner. She and Dan settled on the couch opposite, with the coffee table between them. She nervously adjusted the magazines she always arranged artfully on the table—purely decorative pieces, as she'd explained to Dan long ago when he'd teased her about them.

"Well," Mandie began, "I don't want to waste your time, so let's get straight to it..."

She took the lead, explaining to the Master Arborist how Dan had launched his business and quickly become overwhelmed. Then he'd watched Hank's show and experienced an epiphany about how his business resembled a fruit tree needing pruning and thinning.

Dan admired how thoroughly yet concisely she outlined their situation. She detailed how they'd applied pruning and thinning not only to the business but to their family life as well, offering specific examples before folding her hands in her lap as she concluded.

"We've invited you here to provide further insight into *pruning* and *thinning* because we sense our lives are much more like fruit trees than we realize."

"That's what I've been trying to tell people for years!" Hank exclaimed, slapping his knee and nodding vigorously. "Nature offers countless lessons. It's tragic how disconnected we've become from the land."

He leaned forward, eyes bright. "I could sit here and lecture you all day. But that's not how I teach. Nature teaches by showing, not telling. So let's do this differently." He looked at them both. "I've got a small orchard on my property, about twenty minutes from here. Would you come out and let me show you what I mean? Bring gloves. You're going to get your hands dirty."

Dan looked at Mandie. She was already reaching for her purse.

"Would you mind if we made a video recording?" she asked. "I'll use my phone if that's okay. We won't show it to others without your permission. I just don't want us to forget anything important."

"Absolutely okay. Mind if I get a copy?" Hank asked. "Never know when it'll come in handy for an episode."

"Not at all!" Mandie sprang up from the couch. "I'll be right back!"

Chapter Seven

Hank's orchard sat on a gentle slope behind his farmhouse—several rows of fruit trees stretching across the property, their branches heavy with early-season growth. The afternoon sun was warm, and the air smelled of cut grass and something sweeter underneath.

"Every row out here is the same variety, same age, same soil," Hank said, leading them between the trees. "I've pruned and thinned all of them except that one." He pointed to a row at the far end and they made their way toward it. "Tell me what you see."

Dan looked. The difference was unmistakable. The unpruned trees were thick and tangled—branches crossing over each other, fruit crowded together in clusters small, green, and hard. The trees looked full, even impressive from a distance. But up close, they were struggling under their own growth.

The pruned rows told a different story. Fewer branches, more space between them. The remaining fruit was still immature—hard and small this early in the season—but evenly spaced along each branch, each piece with room to grow. The trees looked spare, almost bare compared to their neighbors. But there was an order to them, a clarity that the tangled row lacked entirely.

"The full trees look more impressive," Dan admitted. "But they're not healthier, are they?"

"They're exhausted," Hank said. "Every branch fighting every other branch for the same water, the same sun, the same nutrients. The fruit never reaches its potential because there's simply too much of it. Come harvest, the pruned row will produce larger, sweeter, better fruit—and more of it by weight—than the tangled row. Less fruit, greater harvest. Every time."

He reached into his belt attachment and lifted out the pruning shears he'd brought. He held them out to Dan.

"Cut that branch." He pointed to a thick secondary branch on one of the unpruned trees—one that crossed over a main limb, blocking light from the fruit beneath it.

Dan took the shears. He hesitated. The branch was alive—it had leaves, it was growing, it even had a healthy row of small hard fruit along its length.

"It looks healthy," Dan said.

"It is healthy," Hank said. "That's what makes it hard. It's not dead wood. It's a living branch that's drawing resources from the branches that matter more. If you leave it, every branch around it produces less. Sometimes the hardest thing to cut is the thing that isn't bad—it's just too much."

Dan positioned the shears and cut. The branch fell to the ground with its leaves still green. He felt the wrongness of it in his hands—removing something alive, something growing. But when he stepped back, he could see the difference immediately. Light reached the fruit beneath. The remaining branches had room to breathe.

Mandie had been watching quietly. "That's my garden society," she said.

Dan and Hank both turned to her.

"It's alive and growing. I enjoy it. It's not a bad thing. But it's taking resources from what matters more." She looked at the fallen branch on the ground. "I need to make that call."

Hank smiled. "Now you're learning what the trees know. The hardest cut isn't removing what's dead. It's removing what's alive but in the way."

They moved down the row, Hank pointing, Dan cutting. With each branch that fell, Dan felt the principle settling deeper. He thought of his problem customers—the ones consuming seventeen percent of his time. Not bad people. Just branches growing in the wrong direction.

Then Hank showed them thinning. He led them to a branch heavy with immature fruit—small hard green spheres clustered together, each competing for the same nourishment.

"Watch," Hank said. He reached in and twisted off fruit after fruit, letting them fall to the ground until only every third or fourth piece remained, evenly spaced along the branch. Over half the fruit lay in the dirt.

"That feels wasteful," Mandie said.

"It feels that way," Hank agreed. "But what remains will grow twice the size and three times the sweetness. Leave everything on the branch and you get a hundred small, hard, bitter fruits. Thin it, and you get forty that are magnificent. Less growth. Greater harvest. The tree knows this. We're the ones who have to learn it."

Dan looked at the fruit on the ground—good fruit, potential fruit, removed so that what remained could become something better. "That's the hardest part," he said. "Letting go of things that aren't bad—just too many."

"Now you understand," Hank said quietly.

They worked for another hour, moving down the rows, cutting and thinning. Hank talked as they worked—not lecturing but conversing, the way a man does when his hands are busy and his mind is free. Mandie recorded snippets on her phone for later review.

"When life becomes overgrown," Hank said, snipping a crossing branch, "your true nature suffocates. Your authentic calling drowns beneath all the things you feel you must do, never allowing your soul to do what it needs to do. As you prune and thin away the excess, your true nature emerges—revealing where and how to grow for maximum harvest."

He paused to examine a branch. "Kids are like young saplings, you know. You plant them and place stakes beside them—the stakes represent parents. The support must be firm enough to prevent bent growth, but loose enough to allow movement in the wind. That freedom lets the roots strengthen. The result? They stand straight and true on their own at maturity."

Mandie caught Dan's eye. He knew she was thinking of their children, of the family council she was planning.

Before they walked back toward the truck, Dan reached up to cut one last high branch and felt a twinge in his chest—brief, sharp, gone almost before he registered it. He lowered his arm and rolled his shoulder.

"You okay?" Mandie asked.

"Fine. Just stretched wrong."

She studied him for a moment, then let it go.

On the drive home, Dan sat with the pruning shears still in his hands. He hadn't meant to keep them. But Hank had noticed and said, "Hold onto those. You'll need them—not for trees."

Dan looked at them and thought about the green branch lying on the ground with its leaves still bright. Sometimes the hardest thing to cut is the thing that isn't bad. It's just too much.

Chapter Eight

Late afternoon sunlight filtered into the garage workshop as Dan added finishing touches to a new figurine—this one a bowler. With countless bowling leagues across the nation, he reasoned there should be a solid market for bowling figurines.

A burst of static broke the stillness—their makeshift intercom system of tourist-style walkie-talkies, with Mandie keeping one in the kitchen and Dan in the garage for easy communication.

Mandie's voice crackled through, "Dan, mail's here with a box for you. I think it's the one you've been waiting for. From that *other* company."

Indeed, he had been anticipating this package—a shipment of competing figurines one of his larger suppliers had mentioned, supposedly selling for 25% less than his prices.

He secured the soldering iron in its stand, switched off the power, double-checked for fire hazards, and headed to the kitchen where he knew Mandie would be waiting.

He found her at their new kitchen table—one of their judicious furniture upgrades as they cautiously saved for a new home. A medium-sized box occupied Dan's usual place, alongside a small knife for cutting the tape. Mandie sat across from him, sorting through the remaining mail.

"Is it what I think it is?" Mandie asked.

Dan examined the label as he took his seat. "It is."

He couldn't suppress the butterflies in his stomach. *This is silly,* he thought. *It will be what it will be.* Still, he couldn't shake the feeling that this box's contents could threaten his livelihood. If these products proved too competitive, matching their price would force him to end his assembly outsourcing to cut costs. It would undo much of his thinning work.

Well, not all of it—just a substantial portion. He'd have to return to round-the-clock work filling orders, unless he outsourced to Mexico. But shipping costs would likely eliminate any savings there.

He glanced at Mandie. She watched him intently, surely sensing his apprehension.

Dan reached into the Styrofoam peanuts and withdrew the first figurine, placing it on the table. Wordlessly, he continued until five figurines stood before him.

They weren't exact copies of his designs. They were similar, but... smaller. Dan studied them in silence.

Mandie rose, disappeared into the front room, and returned with one of Dan's figurines, setting it beside the others.

What a woman, Dan thought. *She went straight to the heart of it*. He looked at her, still silent.

"You don't have a thing to worry about!" Mandie declared. "Just look at them."

And he did. Each figurine was a third smaller, with more fragile, bendable wire gauging. The solder joints, while firm, lacked the clean precision he demanded in his products. Cheap plastic replaced quality materials in the pedestals. Instead of engraved metal strips identifying each piece, they used stickers on the plastic bases.

"I don't think you should discount at all," Mandie said. "For a serious gift, I'd choose your figurines nine times out of ten. No wonder your customers haven't switched to these smaller units. They're not worth it."

"Spoken like a protective Mama Bear," Dan said, exhaling in relief. Mandie was right, but something nagged at him. His business wasn't threatened, but his buyers had clearly been angling for price reductions. Was that all?

He considered contacting them to announce he'd analyzed the competition and would maintain his prices. But that seemed too harsh. He wanted to show good faith while maintaining relationships. But how?

He asked Mandie what she thought.

After they both pondered for a moment, she said, "Well, if you can't beat them, join them."

Dan raised his eyebrows. "What?"

"If your buyers want a lower-priced product, why not provide it?" Mandie gestured at the smaller figurines. "What would it take to create your own version? A self-knockoff? Your suppliers already work with you. If you can produce quality smaller figurines at lower prices, wouldn't they prefer buying from you?"

Understanding dawned on Dan. She was right! "Mandie, did I ever tell you you're a genius?"

"Only every other day," she smiled. "But I never tire of hearing it."

"Well, you are!" Dan's mind raced with potential improvements for the smaller figurines. If he could produce them at 25% less cost, the profit margin would work.

"I'm calling those buyers," he said. "I'll tell them what I've discovered and offer them my full line in two sizes—regular and small, with the smaller ones at 25% less... and better quality than the competition.

"They'll go for it," he continued, thinking aloud. "They want quality merchandise at a lower price point. It fills a different niche than my regular line. I can do better than these," he gestured to the smaller figures.

His excitement mounted. "Instead of threatening the business, this competition opens new opportunities. Dare I say *lower hanging fruit*." He smiled at the pun.

"I need to make those calls and get to the hardware store for prototype supplies. Then I can calculate costs accurately and update the website.

"We could even sell them as sets—matching large and small figurines."

"Hey, before you go," Mandie raised her hand holding an opened letter. "Not to dampen our enthusiasm, but we need to discuss something."

"Oh? What's that?" Dan asked.

"It's an invitation for Dan Jr.," Mandie told Dan. "That basketball coach is asking him again to join their special team. Remember, that's one of the activities we *pruned*."

"Oh-oh," Dan said. "How's that going over?"

"Not well," Mandie sighed. "I'm facing similar issues with the other kids. I sense a mutiny brewing. They keep asking why they can't participate when all their friends do."

"I see what you mean," Dan said. "Should we stand firm?"

"We could, but we'll seem like harsh parents. We already do. I don't want to resort to 'because I said so.'"

"What do you suggest?"

"I've been thinking," Mandie said. "What if we called a family board meeting and explained everything—The Ultimate Investment, The Opportunity Tree, and the Pruning and Thinning principles we've learned? At least they'd understand our reasoning."

Dan paused. "You think they'll grasp it?"

"If we present it at their level."

"You're a Sunday school teacher," Dan said. "If anyone can explain it to them, you can. It's a good idea."

They had limited each child to one sports activity and one music lesson at a time. Initially, the kids had enjoyed their extra home time, mostly watching TV. Then Mandie had introduced reading, games, and outdoor activities, and they'd barely noticed the change.

But now they saw their friends involved in multiple activities, receiving invitations to join... It's hard for children to refuse their friends, especially with fun activities. Yet this was exactly what Dan and Mandie wanted to avoid—over-programmed, over-committed kids.

The children had just started discovering their interests and abilities, growing and flourishing. And now this challenge.

"If they understand, they can help plan. Maybe with more ownership, it'll be easier for them," Mandie suggested.

"That sounds promising if it works," Dan said.

"So it's okay?"

"Absolutely," Dan nodded. "What do you need from me?"

"You handle the business. When I have things to review, we'll discuss them. I want us aligned before we talk to the kids."

"Sounds like I get the easy part as usual, but I don't mind," Dan said, circling the table to kiss her cheek. "I love you, you know."

"You'd better!" Mandie smiled. "Now get going. You have work to do."

Dan laughed as he gathered the smaller figurines back into the packing box. "I'm off to make some calls and visit the hardware store."

#

The next morning, Mandie sat at the kitchen table with her phone. She'd been putting this off for a week, but the branch on the orchard ground kept coming back to her—green leaves, still alive, lying in the dirt because it was in the way of something better.

She dialed.

"Carol? It's Mandie. I'm calling about the Garden Society." She paused. "I need to step down."

The response was immediate and exactly what she'd expected. "But Mandie, you're so good at this. We need you. The summer show is only four weeks away. Can't you stay through the season?"

Mandie looked at the plaque on the wall. "I've loved being part of it, Carol. Truly. But I need to focus on my family right now. I'm spreading myself too thin, and the things that matter most are getting my leftovers."

There was a silence on the line. Then Carol said she understood, though her voice said she didn't. They exchanged pleasantries and hung up.

Mandie set the phone down. She felt guilty—the way Dan had felt cutting that living branch. But she also felt lighter. One less thing pulling resources from the branches that needed to bear fruit.

She picked up her pen and crossed "Garden Society" off her list. Then she looked at the next item and reached for the phone again.

Chapter Nine

"I bet you're all wondering why you've been called here," Mandie said, standing before the TV in their front room where the whole family could see her. Dan sat on the couch with ten-year-old Ronnie snuggled against him. Dan Jr. slouched in the recliner, while Melissa settled on the floor beside Moochie, the family mutt. By unanimous decree, Moochie had to be present at all family meetings.

"This is the first of what will become regular family board meetings. Do you all know what a board meeting is?"

Melissa's hand shot up from her spot on the floor. "Does that mean we're going to be bored?"

Dan chuckled.

"We certainly hope not," Mandie smiled. "A board meeting is where all the leaders of a group gather to decide important things. Since our family is a group, your father and I thought we should all come together to make important decisions."

Dan glanced at fifteen-year-old Dan Jr., who tried to maintain his cool demeanor but clearly perked up at this different approach.

"I thought we might get *hit* with a board," Melissa quipped, embracing her role as the thirteen-year-old family joker.

"I don't want to be hit with a board," Ronnie looked up at Dan with pleading brown eyes.

"No one's getting hit with anything," Dan assured him, pulling him closer. "Maybe we should call this a *family council* meeting instead."

"Yes, that's much better," Mandie agreed. "Today we're going to discuss some important things your father and I have been talking about. We think it's time you kids helped make some family decisions too.

"To begin," she retrieved a tablet computer from the coffee table and turned on the TV, already connected by cable, "I want to share some things that have happened to Mom and Dad. Then we'll talk about how they affect all of us."

Mandie launched into a concise description, complete with PowerPoint presentation and relevant images, of their experience discovering The Ultimate Investment. She held nothing back, though she simplified the story for all age levels. Dan marveled at her teaching ability.

She spoke candidly about Dan's job loss, their search for clues in the library, and a remarkable woman named Elizabeth who had left those clues for them to find. "She taught us the most important lesson of our lives," Mandie told the children, "that time is our most precious investment. And she cared enough about us to let us discover it ourselves, even when it would have been easier to just tell us." She continued with Dan finding and losing another job.

Though the children knew these events, Dan and Mandie had never discussed them openly. Watching their expressions, Dan realized they should have shared more all along. The kids had sensed the problems but, without discussion, had carried their own fears. They'd known their parents were stressed but felt helpless—and stressed themselves.

Dan regretted not seeing this sooner. Regular family councils could have kept the children informed, reassuring them that their parents were working hard to ensure they'd always have a home, food, and love.

Mandie continued, displaying images of a giant fruit tree and other Tree of Life motifs while describing Dan's dream—their

Opportunity Tree. She explained their experiences: Dan following the path, reaching the tree, tasting the fruit, finding success.

Then she addressed the next phase—Dan noticed this particularly resonated with the children—when Dad became overwhelmed with his successful but demanding business.

Dan caught Dan Jr.'s slight unconscious nod and felt a pang of regret. Ronnie snuggled closer.

Dan took a slow breath. His chest felt tight—just for a moment, a flutter that came and went. He attributed it to the emotion of watching Mandie teach their children so beautifully. He pulled Ronnie closer and let the feeling pass.

"But remember how Dad left his work and joined us at Disneyland? Even though he arrived late, he made up for it with an extra day."

"Yay!" Melissa shouted from the floor. "When can we do that again?"

"I think soon," Mandie said, looking at Dan.

He smiled. "Soon."

"Yay!" all three children cheered in unison.

"And do you want to know why we can do that?" Mandie asked.

"Because Dad's making lots of money!" Melissa exclaimed. Moochie, startled by the cheering, darted looks between family members.

"It's okay, Moochie," Melissa soothed, rubbing his head. "This is a good family council! Maybe they'll let you come to Disneyland too." Moochie gazed intently into her eyes.

Dan chuckled. The kids were embracing the family council concept. He hoped they'd grasp the important principles as well as the vacation plans.

Ronnie looked up. "Are we really going to Disneyland again? Will you come too?"

"Yes, we'll go to Disneyland again," Dan assured him. "But not just yet. We have important things to decide first, and we need to save money. We'll plan it later. For now, let's let Mom finish so we can discuss those important things."

On cue, Mandie switched screens. "I have a video for you to watch." The children perked up. "This video explains why Mom and Dad have reduced their activities, and why you children each do one music lesson and one sports activity at a time. Watch carefully, and you'll understand. Then we'll have questions and answers."

"Is it a test?" Dan Jr. asked.

"No. It's not a test. You'll understand when you watch." Mandie started the video—an edited version of the Master Arborist show mixed with clips she'd recorded on her phone.

Dan admired Mandie's editing. The five-and-a-half-minute clip captured all the major points the Master Arborist had shared. When it ended, Mandie turned off the tablet and placed it on the hearth.

"Now for questions. Why did the Master Arborist prune the trees?"

Melissa's hand shot up. "To keep the tree from getting gnarly and overgrown!"

Dan Jr. raised his hand. "So the best branches will grow stronger."

Little Ronnie echoed, "So the best branches will grow stronger!"

"You're all right! Such smart children we have. Now, do you remember about thinning?"

"Yes! So each fruit grows bigger and tastes better," Melissa answered quickly, competitive and bright.

Ronnie raised his hand. "I want to taste!"

"That's exactly right," Mandie smiled. "Now here's a challenging question. Think carefully before answering: How are people like fruit trees?"

"What?" Dan Jr. asked.

"Think about it," Mandie encouraged.

The children fell silent, even Melissa furrowing her brow in concentration. Then Dan Jr. raised his hand.

"I get it. People grow. As they grow, they get bigger and spread out."

"That's right," Mandie said slowly. "But keep thinking. Remember how Dad's business became gnarly and overgrown, taking all his time until he almost missed Disneyland?"

"Oh yeah," Melissa said. Moochie lifted his head to stare at her.

"And why we've limited you each to one sports activity and one music lesson at a time?"

"You don't want us to get gnarly and overgrown, right?" Melissa concluded. Dan marveled at her quick understanding. He'd need to watch more closely for her growing wisdom.

Dan spoke up. "That's right. Dad *pruned* some work activities and thinned others. I've created systems to work less while earning more. Though I do less personally, everything I do has more value and quality."

"So you're helping us all grow bigger and better by pruning and thinning our lives like Dad did with his business?" Dan Jr. asked.

"Exactly right!" Mandie beamed. "We're working to improve as a whole family. Danny, consider this: Would you be as good at soccer if you had basketball practice too?

"And Melissa, could you master the flute while taking violin lessons?"

Dan could see the lesson taking root.

"To excel at what matters most to us, we must prune and thin away things we might enjoy but aren't as important."

"Oh, I get it," Melissa said, still rubbing Moochie's belly.

"So when we discuss limiting activities and spending more family time, we're really pruning and thinning our lives to grow better as a family and as individuals."

Dan admired how effectively Mandie had conveyed these principles. The children truly understood.

"Your father and I thought," Mandie continued, "we could hold family council meetings every few months. We'll evaluate our progress and adjust what we're pruning and thinning from our lives. This ensures we're all growing in ways most important to each of us."

"Like Disneyland!" Melissa shouted. Moochie lifted his head again. "It's okay, Moochie. Mom's just teaching us how to be good-tasting fruit!"

Chapter Ten

Late one evening, Dan sat in his garage workshop updating system notes and customer order progress charts on his laptop. The kids were in bed, and Mandie was finishing the dinner cleanup. He wanted to use this quiet time to better systematize his new line of smaller figurines.

He'd uploaded photos and sales information to the website and delivered the first prototypes and materials to his assemblers, who had begun work on the initial batch of orders.

Recent thinning efforts had streamlined his ordering, assembly, fulfillment, billing, and payment systems. Everything operated electronically now, thanks to Mandie's help. Her growing computer expertise matched her organizational skills—no wonder their home always ran so smoothly.

At Mandie's suggestion, Dan had also outsourced shipping to a professional company. Though it cost more than handling it himself, Mandie had pointed out that his *time* held greater value. Others could manage packing and shipping, probably more efficiently. But only Dan could handle design and business development.

Now he primarily oversaw operations: downloading orders, assigning work, delivering merchandise to the shipping company, and having raw materials for the assemblers. Life had found its rhythm.

With more time and mental energy, Dan could focus on brainstorming designs and exploring future growth opportunities— the aspects he loved and excelled at.

Dan attended recitals and games again. They'd held two more family councils since the first. The kids looked forward to them now—even Dan Jr. had started bringing his own ideas about how to invest his time better.

His thoughts drifted to where it all began, reflecting on their journey. Despite its difficulties and stresses, it had proved worthwhile.

Now he could concentrate on building and growing, following the "formula" he and Mandie had established—continuing to prune and thin as they progressed.

Their Opportunity Tree bore fruit abundantly. Like a mature fruit tree, it required less intensive "time" to produce its bountiful harvest.

Dan leaned back contentedly in his chair, hands clasped behind his head. His gaze drifted to the framed photo Mandie had given him—Dan and Dan Jr. holding up the first figurine Dan had ever made, the soccer player he'd crafted for his son's birthday. That one small piece of bent wire had started all of this. He smiled at the memory.

Suddenly, tightness gripped his chest. A heavy weight settled there. He couldn't breathe, and his left arm went numb. Pain shot through his shoulder. Sweat broke out on his face as his body turned clammy.

He tried calling out, attempted to reach the walkie-talkie, but couldn't move. His vision began dimming.

Was this how it ended—alone in the garage, with the photo of his son on the shelf and the work of his hands all around him? All the time he'd invested, all the paths he'd walked, and it comes down to this? "Not now!" Dan cried, his voice barely a whisper. "Please—not now."

His vision continued fading as he felt himself falling into a deep pit.

Chapter Eleven

Dan awakened slowly, sensing something wasn't right. He couldn't place his surroundings. His eyes fluttered open to blurry vision and unfamiliar surroundings.

Then he felt a hand grasp his.

"You're awake." Mandie's voice.

He turned toward the sound, recognizing her familiar outline. A faint smile crossed his lips. "Where am I? What happened?"

Mandie leaned down to kiss his forehead. "I'm so glad you're back with us. You've been drifting in and out. You just had surgery."

"Surgery?"

"Yes. Do you remember anything?"

Dan struggled through the fog. "I... was working in the garage. And then... everything's hazy. Things went dark. Oh yes, chest pain and my arm went numb." He looked at Mandie. "Did I...?"

"Yes, Dan, you had a heart attack. The blockage was severe. You'd been ignoring warning signs, hadn't you? The shoulder aches, the chest tightness—I noticed at the orchard, Dan. I noticed at the family council. I should have pushed harder." Anger and relief mingled in her voice.

Dan remained silent. She was right.

"You've undergone a quintuple bypass."

"A what?"

"A quintuple bypass. We almost lost you. The doctor says your disorientation and memory gaps are normal."

Dan's vision had cleared enough to see tears streaming down Mandie's face.

"I don't remember any of it."

"You will, according to the doctor. Thank goodness it happened at home and I found you quickly. The ambulance arriving terrified the kids."

"The kids?"

"They're with your parents, and they know you'll be alright."

"So I will be alright?"

Mandie smiled, caressing his face and squeezing his hand. "Yes, you'll be alright."

Chapter Twelve

Three days after the surgery, at six in the morning, Mandie sat in Dan's workshop chair. The laptop was open, the order system glowing on the screen. Her manila folder lay beside it, and on the shelf above the desk, Elizabeth's leather-bound notebook stood between two figurines like a bookend.

She'd been here every morning since the ambulance. Processing orders, assigning work to the assemblers, answering customer emails. The systems Dan had built through pruning and thinning—the automated ordering, the independent contractors, the streamlined shipping—held firm without him. She was maintaining them, not rebuilding them. That was the difference. That was what the thinning had been for.

The phone rang. A customer with a question about delivery timing on the new smaller figurines.

"Dan's Designs, this is Mandie," she said, and heard her own voice—calm, professional, sure. Two years of business coursework and a year of watching Dan build this company had prepared her for exactly this moment. She just hadn't known it.

She answered the customer's question, confirmed the shipping date, and hung up. Then she heard footsteps—small ones, shuffling—and turned to find Ronnie in the doorway in his pajamas, holding a mug with both hands.

"I made you coffee," he said. "Like you make for Dad."

Mandie took the mug. It was mostly milk with a little coffee, lukewarm, and it was the best cup she'd ever been given. She pulled Ronnie onto her lap and held him for a moment, looking at the screen, the orders, the work of her husband's hands arranged on shelves around her. The business was alive. The family was holding. The tree was sheltering them, just as they'd pruned it to do.

#

"When can I leave?" Dan asked.

Mandie sat beside his hospital bed. After five days, his patience wore increasingly thin.

"I want to go home. I want to see the kids."

They'd allowed the children one visit to assure themselves of his recovery.

"If you behave, the doctor says you can leave tomorrow. Your vitals look good, and your strength is returning. You're up and driving everyone crazy—that's promising."

"Great," Dan said.

"You remember what happened?"

Dan paused. "I remember worrying most about you and the kids when everything went dark. I didn't want to leave you. And yes, I remember arriving here, the surgery, all of it."

Mandie squeezed his hand, tears forming in both their eyes.

"None of that," Dan said. "I'm going home tomorrow."

"Only if you promise to be a good patient and rest properly." Her voice was stern despite her smile.

Dan fell silent. A question had nagged him for days, but he'd feared the answer. He couldn't avoid it now. They both needed to face it.

"I've been afraid to ask, but... what about the business?"

"The business is thriving under its new manager."

"What? Who?"

Mandie's smile widened. "Me.

"While you've been here, I've handled everything—delivering materials to assemblers, processing orders and payments, even speaking with customers.

"I emailed most of them about your heart attack and surgery, assuring them operations would continue normally.

"They all send their best wishes. And they *love* the new manager." She grinned.

"Wow. Are you managing okay? I'm sorry to put you in this position. I'll try to return soon."

"No need. I actually enjoy it. Remember when I started that first business management course? You told me 'That's not a third thing. That's the whole point.' Well—this is what it was for. I just didn't know it yet. Though circumstances forced my hand, I'd like to continue growing in this direction—if you don't mind."

"Do I have a choice?"

"You're still CEO and chief designer, but no, you don't. Besides, I like the title of Chief Operating Officer better. It fits with what I like to do.

"Since we pruned and thinned the business and automated most processes, it's been surprisingly manageable. I've focused mainly on launching the new product line according to your vision.

"And then... I tried some things." For the first time, Mandie looked uncertain.

"What? Should I worry?"

"Actually no, but I'm not sure how to tell you."

"Tell me what? Is everything okay?"

"Well..." Mandie said. "Remember my mentioning customer conversations? I asked them for rep recommendations to expand our outlets." Her expression turned peculiar.

"What did you do?"

"I couldn't help myself. I contacted them, narrowed it to two promising candidates, and sent them website links. They loved our products and want to represent them. They're drafting standard agreements and believe they can each add twenty shops—forty new accounts!"

"Wow!" Dan processed this news. Then smiled. "I've hired an amazing COO!"

"The best part," Mandie said, relief evident at his approval, "our systems can handle it. We'll only need more assemblers. Everything else is ready.

"You just focus on designing—limited, of course, until you're fully recovered."

"I'd like that," Dan said, then fell quiet.

"Are you angry?" Mandie asked.

Dan squeezed her hand and smiled. "Not angry. Proud!"

"This is exciting," Mandie said. "Invigorating. I know to keep growth slow and steady, so we don't let the tree become overgrown—with me being the overgrown one this time."

"Everything seems under control. I guess I can rest." Dan felt a twinge of sadness, as if becoming redundant in his own company.

"Remember the Master Arborist saying pruning and thinning traumatizes the tree but forces it to draw greater strength from its roots and accelerate growth? I hate to say it, but one of our final pruning tasks was reducing *your* integral role in the business." Mandie watched him carefully.

"Fortunately, we'd completed automation and systematization just before your attack, making it easy for me to step in. That pruning and thinning allowed the Opportunity Tree to shelter our family. Without those changes, that same tree would have crushed us."

They sat in thoughtful silence. Dan recognized the blessing of following the right path... of pruning and thinning. Mandie was right.

"Besides, I've learned so much about myself," Mandie broke the silence. "I love being more involved in the business. I'm grateful you always kept me informed. That saved us!"

"And you saved me!" Dan said.

He realized then that his Ultimate Investment's greatest return wasn't the business. It was the love he shared with his wife and children. No success could taste sweeter than that.

Chapter Thirteen

"This opens the first Executive Committee Meeting of Dan's Designs." Dan spoke with mock solemnity, staring across the table at Mandie, the only other member of the executive committee.

Mandie smiled, glancing around. They sat in a library—but this one graced a cruise ship sailing the Mediterranean Sea. Picture windows offered a panoramic view of the ocean and distant islands softened by a blue, sunny haze.

"This is what I call an Executive Committee Meeting," Mandie said.

"Well, I figured since the business was under such good *management*, we should do this annually. You know, to plan stuff." Dan smiled at Mandie. "And then have a family council once a year somewhere fun with the kids."

"So moved!" Mandie said. "What's the next order of business?" She batted her eyelashes.

Fully recovered now, Dan loved his role as CEO and chief designer. Mandie served as COO (Chief Operating Officer)—and excelled at it. The business thrived.

The kids were with his parents. He hoped everyone was surviving.

"For this meeting," Dan said, "I thought we could review our journey, then discuss our future direction."

"Our journey's been quite a ride," Mandie said. "But definitely rewarding."

"Amen to that," Dan agreed. "To think it all began with finding a note in a library." He looked around. "Libraries have held special significance for us."

"Indeed they have," Mandie said.

"That first note led us to search for The Ultimate Investment," Dan mused. "How do you think we've handled that investment?"

Mandie gazed around the room, then out to sea. "I'd say pretty well."

"Elizabeth was right. The Ultimate Investment made all the difference."

"Then came the Opportunity Tree," Dan continued. "That dream arrived precisely when we needed it most. It helped us focus our Ultimate Investment on the right path. You know the saying's true: 'follow the path, live the dream'—and yes, the pun was intended."

"Now about the future," Dan said.

"What about it?" Mandie asked.

"Subject to you and the kids' approval," Dan said, "I want to try something new."

"Something new?"

"Yes. It relates to the Opportunity Tree dream. I've been thinking about its ending. It hasn't fully manifested yet."

"I remember discussing that," Mandie said. "You mentioned 'the journey wasn't over.' What are you thinking?"

"In the dream," Dan explained, "I gathered seeds and found a large field with fertile soil. I planted those seeds and grew another Opportunity Tree."

"I thought we were doing that," Mandie said. "Aren't we?"

"One could see it that way. Or perhaps we're still enjoying fruit from the original Opportunity Tree. Our pruning and thinning focused on that first tree—that initial opportunity—which bears substantial fruit.

"We could take those seeds to new territory, explore different opportunities, plant them, and grow another Opportunity Tree."

"And..." Mandie prompted.

"I've been developing designs beyond figurines—unique wind vanes with special movements forming different images as the wind flows through them. Darrel shows talent in this area, and I've enlisted his help brainstorming ideas. It's a completely different market. Paul thinks the festival circuit would be ideal for the wind vanes—different customer, same distribution model. He's already sketched out a launch plan.

"They'd command higher prices and attract different buyers through new outlets—home and garden stores, nurseries, internet sales.

"Yet the manufacturing process remains similar enough to integrate with our current operations without major disruption. We'd start small, letting it grow naturally like the figurine business.

"This time Darrel would lead design, with my support. He'd receive partial ownership and share in this new Opportunity Tree's growth."

"Wow," Mandie said. "I like that. We have the *time* now, and we know the path."

"One more thing regarding expansion. Dan Jr. has expressed interest in becoming an assembler, eventually moving into design. We should make room for his growth. I think he could develop some excellent ideas."

"If he follows the path, he'll live his dream," Mandie smiled. "So he finally approached you?"

"You knew?"

"Of course. I am the COO, after all."

"Let's add this to our next family council agenda," Dan said. "The whole family should decide about this new opportunity."

"I agree," Mandie said. "Think we'll face any objections?"

"Not if we invest our *Ultimate Investment* wisely," Dan said. "And maintain proper *pruning* and *thinning* as our new *Opportunity Tree* grows."

"One more thing," Dan said. "We're moving to a new house. You'll need a new plaque."

Mandie smiled. She'd been thinking about this. "I want all three lines burned into the wood this time. The paper note is at the end of its life."

"Three lines?"

"We need a third. Something that captures what we've learned about pruning and thinning—the way the first two captured time and the path."

Dan looked out at the Mediterranean, thinking. "It has to be simple. Elizabeth's wisdom was always simple."

"Prune and Thin Annually," Mandie said.

Dan turned to her. Three words and a frequency. An instruction you could read every morning while pouring coffee and carry with you all year. He thought of the orchard—the shears in his hand, the green branch falling, the fruit given room to grow. That's what those four words contained.

"Three lines," he said. "Three milestones of transformation."

Mandie pulled a napkin toward her and wrote it down in her careful hand, the way she'd written everything since the night she'd first pinned seven words to a refrigerator. "Elizabeth would have approved," she said.

They fell silent. Dan looked around again. "You know, I've really grown to love libraries!"

Chapter Fourteen

"I can't believe all that's happened!" Dan surveyed the empty front room. The house stood bare, stripped clean. They'd donated the old furniture to goodwill; barely anything would join them in their new home, nearly triple this size. He shook his head. *Such transformation. I haven't worked harder—less actually. But with more effectiveness, more passion.* Dan contemplated the difference.

Mandie and the kids were arranging furniture at the new house. Only the old family portrait remained, hanging slightly askew at Dan's request. He'd sent the family ahead for some quiet reflection time, to look around and say goodbye.

He smiled. *Strange to feel so attached to this house. I didn't even like it initially. Yet here I stand—new business, new life, new home.*

Dan approached the picture frame, grasped its sides, and lifted it from its hook.

Then he walked to the kitchen. The plaque was still on the wall—the last thing remaining besides the portrait. Mandie's burned lettering on the first line, the paper note taped beneath it with edges curling after years of kitchen heat and morning light. He lifted it carefully from its nail and held both objects—the portrait in one hand, the plaque in the other. Two things that told the whole story of who they'd been in this house.

"So much has happened," he addressed the images. "If I hadn't lived it, I wouldn't believe it. And it all began with a simple investment—The Ultimate Investment."

Dan closed his eyes, gentle tears tracing his cheeks. Elizabeth had been right. Simple yet powerful. The Ultimate Investment meant investing in life's fullness.

Dan cradled the picture and plaque in his arms, opened his eyes, and gazed around the empty room. "The end of one life and beginning of another started here. Now for a new chapter..." He walked from the kitchen to the front door, switched off the light, and pulled it shut behind him.

Chapter Fifteen

That evening, before the children went to bed, Mandie called everyone to the kitchen of the new house. Dan leaned against the doorframe, watching. The kids gathered around the island, curious.

Mandie held up a wooden plaque—new, freshly crafted, the wood smooth and light. She'd been working on it for days, burning the letters with the same careful hand that had lettered the first plaque years ago in a kitchen they no longer owned. But this one had three lines, not two. All burned into the wood. All permanent.

Invest your time. Don't just spend it.

Follow the Path, Live the Dream.

Prune and Thin Annually.

She hung it on the wall beside the new refrigerator, at eye level, and stepped back. Dan came up beside her. The kids gathered around them. They all stood reading it together—the way Dan and Mandie had once stood reading a single line in a different kitchen, in a different life.

"What does 'prune and thin' mean again?" Ronnie asked.

"It means cutting away what's in the way," Melissa said, "so the good stuff can grow. Like at Hank's orchard. Remember?"

"Three lines," Dan Jr. said quietly. "That's your whole story, isn't it?"

Dan looked at his eldest son and felt something shift in his chest—not pain this time, but pride. "That's our whole story," he said.

Then Mandie reached into her pocket and pulled out a folded piece of paper. She held it out to Dan. "Your updated edition," she said.

Dan unfolded it. Three lines in her careful handwriting. He took out his wallet, slid the old note from behind his driver's license—two lines, creased and softened from years of carrying—and replaced it with the new one. The old note he tucked into Mandie's manila folder, beside the silk swatch and Elizabeth's notebook. Nothing lost. Just carried forward.

#

Late that night, Dan sat at his new home office desk. Darkness filled the room except for a desk lamp casting its confined glow downward. He was in pajamas, having come down from the bedroom. Something had been nagging at him for weeks—a restless thought insisting on attention. Tonight it grew impossible to ignore.

He sat within the lamp's pool of light. On the shelf behind the desk stood the framed photo of Dan and Dan Jr. holding the first figurine. Beside it, Elizabeth's leather-bound notebook, its cover worn smooth from years of handling. And through the open doorway, if he turned his head, he could see the new plaque on the kitchen wall—three lines, faintly visible in the hallway light.

He opened a drawer, withdrew paper and pen, and placed them before him. He leaned back, contemplating. Writing always helped organize his thoughts.

Dan grasped the pen and touched it to paper. Nothing came. He closed his eyes, emptying his mind, breathing deeply.

The thought emerged—easing into his consciousness with such gentleness it reminded him of someone long gone. A woman with a cane, sitting in a wingback chair, who had refused to give him the answer because she loved him too much to make it easy. Who had left clues in a library for a stranger she'd never met, trusting that someone would come.

Now Dan was the one with something to pass on. He didn't know who would find it. He didn't know when. But he knew, with a certainty that settled into his bones like warmth, that it was time.

Dan smiled. "I get the message, Elizabeth," he spoke into the darkness, then leaned into the lamp's glow and began to write.

Dear Friend:

If you're reading this letter, then you need my help...

The End

Appendix
Thinning Your Life Workbook
A Practical Guide to Pruning and Thinning for a Richer Life

A Note Before You Begin

If you've just finished Thinning Your Life, you've watched Dan and Mandie face a crisis they never expected — not failure, but success that was consuming them. You've stood with Dan in Hank's orchard, holding the pruning shears, cutting a living branch because it was in the way of something better. And you've watched Mandie run a business from a workshop chair at six in the morning with a cup of mostly-milk coffee from her youngest son.

The first two books in this series taught you what to invest (your time) and what to invest it in (work you love). This book — and this workbook — teaches you how to protect what you've built by regularly cutting away what doesn't serve it.

Pruning and thinning isn't a one-time fix. Trees need it every year. So do lives. That's why the third line on the plaque reads:

Prune and Thin Annually.

This workbook gives you the tools to do exactly that — in your work, your finances, your relationships, your health, and your personal growth. Hank taught Dan and Mandie in the orchard; this workbook is your orchard.

Let's begin.

Section One: The Pruning Principle

Pruning means eliminating activities, commitments, and obligations that don't align with your core purposes — or that actively impede them. It's the hardest part of thinning your life, because the things you need to cut are often alive and growing. They're not bad. They're just in the way.

> *Hank pointed to a thick secondary branch that crossed over a main limb, blocking light from the fruit beneath it. "It looks healthy," Dan said. "It is healthy," Hank replied. "That's what makes it hard."*

How to Identify What Needs Pruning

Ask yourself these questions about each major commitment in your life:

Does this serve my core purpose? If not, it's a candidate for pruning — no matter how enjoyable or impressive it seems.

Is this drawing resources from what matters more? Time, energy, and attention are finite. Every branch that grows takes nourishment from every other branch. What is this commitment taking from?

Would I start this today? If you wouldn't begin this commitment knowing what you know now, that's a strong signal it needs to go.

The 80/20 test: Does this fall in the 20% that produces 80% of my results? Or the 80% that produces only 20%? Dan discovered his problem customers represented less than 1% of

volume but consumed 17% of his time. That's a branch that needs cutting.

Your Pruning Inventory

List your major commitments — work, personal, community, family. For each one, note whether it serves your core purpose and whether you'd start it today.

Commitment	Serves Core Purpose?	Would Start Today?	Action

The commitments where you answered "No" to both questions are your pruning priorities. Remember Mandie calling the show society president: the guilt is real, but so is the relief. Cut the living branch so the fruit-bearing ones can grow.

Section Two: The Thinning Principle

Thinning is different from pruning. Pruning removes what doesn't belong. Thinning streamlines what remains — creating systems, delegating, simplifying — so your core activities can be accomplished with greater ease, less stress, and better results.

> *Hank reached in and twisted off fruit after fruit until only every third piece remained, evenly spaced along the branch. "What remains will grow twice the size and three times the sweetness."*

Systems: The Heart of Thinning

A system is any repeatable process that accomplishes a core activity more consistently, quickly, and economically — freeing your time and energy for other critical work, or simply for reduced stress and more family time.

Dan's systems saved his family when his heart attack struck. The automated ordering, the independent contractors, the streamlined shipping — all held firm without him. Mandie maintained the systems; she didn't have to rebuild them. That's what thinning does: it makes your life resilient.

Areas to Thin

Work: What tasks do you repeat daily that could be automated, delegated, or simplified? Dan outsourced assembly to independent contractors. Mandie systematized ordering and shipping. What's your equivalent?

Finances: What financial complexity could be simplified? Automatic payments, consolidated accounts, a monthly review ritual instead of constant worry?

Health: What health habits are overcomplicated? Could your exercise routine be simpler but more consistent? Could meal planning reduce daily decisions?

Relationships: Which relationships drain energy without nourishing you? Which ones deserve more of your time? Pruning toxic connections isn't cruel — it's the same principle as the orchard.

Schedule: Where is your calendar overgrown? What meetings, events, and recurring commitments could be thinned so the ones that remain get your full attention?

Section Three: The Annual Review

Trees need pruning every year because they keep growing. So do lives. New commitments creep in. Old habits return. The calendar fills back up. That's natural — it's what living things do. The discipline isn't in pruning once; it's in pruning annually.

Prune and Thin Annually.

Dan and Mandie committed to an annual "Executive Committee Meeting" — a dedicated time to review their business, their family, and their lives with fresh eyes. They also held regular family councils to keep the children engaged in the process.

Here is a framework for your own annual review:

Step 1: Survey the Orchard

Look at your life as Hank looked at his trees. What's overgrown? Where are branches crossing? Where is fruit crowded so tightly it can't mature? Be honest. The tree can't lie about its condition, and neither should you.

What has become overgrown since my last review?

Step 2: Prune

Identify the branches that need to go. Use the pruning inventory from Section One. Remember: the hardest cuts are the living branches — the good things that are crowding out the great things.

What will I prune this year?

Step 3: Thin

Streamline what remains. Create or improve one system. Delegate one task. Simplify one process. You don't have to overhaul everything — just thin enough to give the remaining fruit room to grow.

What will I thin or systematize this year?

Step 4: Nurture What Remains

After pruning and thinning, the remaining branches need extra attention. Give your core commitments — the ones you kept — the time, energy, and focus they deserve. This is where the harvest grows.

What core commitments will I invest more time in this year?

Step 5: Schedule the Next Review

Put next year's review on your calendar now. Make it a ritual — an annual appointment with yourself (and your partner, if you have one) to look at the orchard with honest eyes.

My next annual review date: _____

Section Four: The Plaque

Dan and Mandie's plaque grew with them across three books and three lifetimes' worth of learning. The first line was burned into wood during their darkest hour. The second was taped on as paper, earning its permanence over a year of struggle. The third was written on a cruise ship napkin and burned into a new plaque for a new home.

Three lines. Three books. A complete philosophy for a well-lived life:

**Invest your time. Don't just spend it.
Follow the Path, Live the Dream.
Prune and Thin Annually.**

A Final Word

Dan sat at his desk late at night, in the lamplight, and began to write a letter to a stranger he would never meet. He did it because a woman named Elizabeth had done the same thing for him — leaving clues in a library, trusting that someone would come. The chain of wisdom doesn't end with you reading these words. It continues when you live them – and pass them on.

Elizabeth taught Dan and Mandie to invest their time. They learned to follow the path. Hank showed them how to prune and thin so the harvest could sweeten. And now, at the end of three books, the plaque on the wall says everything that needs to be said.

Your time is your most precious resource. Find work you love and follow that path with everything you have. And every year — every single year — step back, look at your life the way Hank looked at his orchard, and cut away what's in the way of what matters most.

The fruit that remains will be magnificent.

Invest your time. Don't just spend it.

Follow the Path, Live the Dream.

Prune and Thin Annually.

If you liked this book, then you'll love, "The Secrets of Succes: Amazing Achievement from Small and Simple Things."

See other works by H. Bradley Stucki at www.amazon.com/author/hbstucki. Free downloads are often available. Click "Follow" on his Author Page for updates on new releases.

About the Author:

H. Bradley Stucki has been a director in three different investment companies, a Senior Vice President at a bank, and owns three businesses.

He helped pioneer the concept of "Business Incubation" and worked with over 250 fledgling companies helping them grow and flourish while still early in his career.

He was born and raised in southern Utah with horses, cows, and other assorted pets. He is the third of six children and survived childhood only by utilizing an active imagination. His hobbies include reading and travel. He and his wife live in a high mountain valley. Population 200.